Mom,
Thanks for
taught me

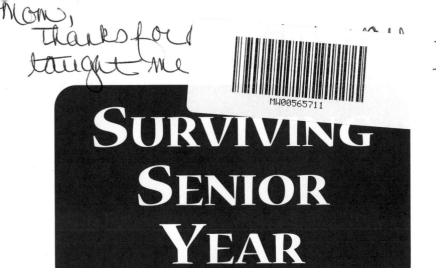

SURVIVING
SENIOR
YEAR

parent

A Parent's Guide to
Successfully Navigating
Your Child's Last Year
of High School

Linda B. Keene

Beaver's Pond Press, Inc.

Edina, Minnesota

Production Supervisor: Milt Adams
Cover and Interior Design: Mori Studio, Inc.

ISBN 1-890676-73-X

Library of Congress Catalog Card Number: 00-107637

Printed in the United States of America

First Printing: September 2000

03 02 01 00   5 4 3 2 1

TABLE OF CONTENTS

Into the Home Stretch:
The Spring Semester

The Grand Finale:
Ceremonies and Celebrations

Transitioning:
The Summer After the Senior Year

LATE JUNE–JULY

AUGUST–EARLY SEPTEMBER

Appendix

ACKNOWLEDGEMENTS

It would not be possible to thank all of the people who have contributed in various ways to my dream of writing a book, but I would like to mention just a few who have touched my life in special ways:

- My parents, Walter and Gertrude Baker, who gave me the confidence to pursue my dreams and who were excellent role models for responsible parenting;

- My husband, Bob, who is my best friend and "the wind beneath my wings" in all that I have accomplished personally and professionally during the past 26 years. Special thanks to his parents, William and Doris Keene, for raising a terrific son and for always treating me like a daughter;

- My son, Jason, a wonderful young man who has always inspired me to try my best as a parent;

- My brother, Brian, and my sister, Michele, who have allowed me to grow from a "big sister" into a friend;

- Our extended family and friends, who form the "village" that has supported Bob and I in our parenting efforts over the years. Special thanks to the "Minnesota Mafia" who have embraced our son as if he were their own;

- My fellow Moms from the Breck School Class of 1999, who contributed many ideas and suggestions to this project. Special thanks to Debbie Stofer, who really went the extra mile in encouraging me to write this book, and to Nancy Proman, for always being there to coach me through new experiences.

- My new friend and publishing mentor, Milt Adams, who helped make the movie in my mind a reality.

INTRODUCTION

When my son, Jason, began his senior year of high school, I knew that our family was about to experience many new and exciting challenges. But I was totally unprepared for the sheer volume of activity and the many unwritten—and sometimes unspoken—expectations of students and their parents. Although there are many sources of information about applying to college, there were few resources available to help us understand the general flow of what happens during the senior year and how to stay ahead of the game.

If not for the advice and guidance of friends who had traveled this path before me, I would never have been able to get through the process with my sanity intact.

By the time graduation rolled around, I finally had things under control. I had even developed something of a reputation for my "senior year organizing skills." When I had time to reflect, I felt like I had completed a marathon. And like any successful marathoner, I had learned many things that would help me do it better the next time around. As the mother of an only child, there was little opportunity for me to put this knowledge into practice—so I decided to begin sharing it with others on an informal basis.

Over time, I received numerous calls from parents of prospective high school seniors. The subject of these calls was always the same: what could I tell them about the process that would help ensure that their family did not experience unnecessary turmoil during the upcoming year? After speaking with a number of parents one-on-one, I decided that it would be a lot more efficient to get my thoughts down on paper.

Although this guidebook contains references to the college application process, it is not intended as a primary resource in that area. Rather, it is a collection of tips on how to make

1

your student's senior year run more smoothly. The advice is organized according to the academic calendar, with specific suggestions to follow for each month. To supplement my own experiences and research, I have surveyed academic advisors and parents of other recent graduates who were more than willing to share their ideas.

I am pleased to share this first edition of *Surviving Senior Year*, and look forward to any feedback that you would like to provide. Most of all, I hope that it is helpful to you and your family in navigating what promises to be an exciting year.

Getting Ready:

THE SUMMER PRECEDING SENIOR YEAR

The first thing you need to understand is that the senior year of high school goes by FAST! It seems like the whole year proceeds at an accelerated pace. The time between the start of school in September and Christmas Break is just a blur. And you go from there to Spring Break and Graduation in the blink of an eye. One of the first things that experienced parents stress is the importance of using the summer before the senior year to get a head start on some important activities. If you use this time wisely, you and your student can approach the year in a somewhat more relaxed fashion.

SENIOR PHOTOS

✔ Many high schools have adopted the practice of having seniors supply their own portraits, rather than having them taken at school. If this applies in your case, you'll need to make an appointment for your student to have their senior portrait taken ASAP. It is helpful to get this out of the way during July or August if at all possible. Good photographers book up fast and most schools want the photos no later than mid-October.

✔ You will also want to find out how much flexibility your school allows in terms of the style of senior portrait your student can submit. Many young people today prefer an informal pose in casual clothing to the more formal portrait that used to be the standard. Even if this is what your student chooses for the yearbook, it is a good idea to have a traditional "head shot" in dress clothing taken at the same time. This can usually be done at minimal cost, since most photographers offer standard package deals on senior portraits that include several poses. Order extra black & white prints in the wallet size at the same time you place your order for color prints. Black & white is often the preferred format for yearbooks and other print vehicles (e.g. newspapers, magazines, freshman picture books, etc.).

Hint: Be sure to investigate the options provided by the instant photography studios in your area. One of the main advantages of going this route is that they offer great flexibility in putting together the poses and packages that you want—at a lower cost than traditional portrait photographers. Some will even allow you to purchase the negatives, so you can make additional copies at your own convenience.

SELECTING COLLEGES

✔ Have your student begin to narrow their list of college choices. There are a number of excellent research tools available on the Web that can help your student identify schools that might be a good match. These search tools collect the student's preferences on a variety of dimensions and use this information to screen their college database for schools with the desired profile. Most of the tools also contain links to the individual college websites, so your student can easily do additional research on the colleges that are of most interest. The amount and type of information that is available on-line is truly amazing— even including "virtual tours" of many campuses. Encourage your student to use these resources to expand the range of options they might consider. A list of resources to assist you and your student in the college selection and admissions process is provided on page 63.

> **Hint**: One of the advantages of using the on-line search tools is that they can help your student understand that there are a variety of schools that can meet their needs. Too often, students get the idea that they can only be happy at one particular school—which can lead to disappointment if they do not get in. Do everything possible to help them keep an open mind.

✔ One of the most important things you can do to assist your student in the selection process is to have an open discussion of any issues that would be "deal breakers" for you in terms of their attending a particular college. For example, if a college is too expensive for your budget, you need to be clear that their ability to attend would be contingent on receiving enough scholarship assistance to make up the difference. By sharing this information early on and agreeing on a list of schools that you can fully support, you can avoid the unpleasantness that can arise when your student is accepted at a school that you are unwilling (or unable) to have them attend.

> **Hint**: Once you have addressed the "deal breakers," stand back as far as you can from the decision-making. There are many good schools and many good choices for your student. The student's chances for success are best if they own the final decision.

✔ The number of schools a student applies to is a matter of personal choice, although the time and expense involved ($25 - $50 per application) usually results in students and their families setting realistic limits. The consensus of most experts is that the list should include the following:

- 1-2 "safety" schools, where your child is almost certain to be admitted based on the typical profile of students (e.g. grades, test scores, etc.);

- 2-5 "strong possibilities," where your student is well positioned vs. the requirements, but may face a more competitive admissions pool;

- At least 1 "stretch" school, where your student may place at the lower end of the range, but could qualify because of a unique talent or perspective they may bring to the student body.

✔ More than eight schools feels like overkill. If your student is realistic in assessing their skills against the three categories listed above, they should have an excellent chance of being admitted to one or more of the schools on their list.

✔ If time and budget permit, you may also want to schedule some campus visits during the summer. Try to do this when summer school is in session, so that your student can have an opportunity to sit in on classes and get a better feel for the campus atmosphere.

> **Hint**: Encourage your student to speak with other students from your area who attend the colleges they are interested in. If you do not have personal contacts, the college admissions office can put you in touch with local students and recent alumni who would be willing to talk to your student about their school.

SENIOR YEAR MONEY MANAGEMENT

✔ Sit down with your student and have a frank discussion about senior year expenses, many of which will be new items to the family budget. Make a list of the potential expenses and decide together on what the priorities are. For example, college application fees would be higher on the list than buying a new outfit for the senior dance. Let them know exactly what you are willing—and able—to pay for. Be explicit about any contributions you expect your student to make from their part-time or summer earnings. A list of some of the major expense items is provided on page 66.

✔ If you have not already done so, give your student the opportunity to manage their own money during their senior year. This will give them experience in budgeting that will be helpful both in college and later life. As adults, they will have to live within a certain amount of income. The sooner they become accustomed to this idea, the better off they—and you—will be. Once you decide on the amount of money that you will provide for their expenses, give it to them in a lump sum and let them practice making financial tradeoffs. We started out by giving Jason his allowance on a monthly basis in his sophomore year. During his junior and senior years, we progressed to giving it to him on a semester basis—a practice that we have continued now that he is in college.

> **Hint**: Don't try to over-manage your student's choices, and let them live with the consequences. Even though Jason had some challenges handling this responsibility early on, he soon learned that it was no fun to end up with "more month than money." He has become an excellent money manager who rarely asks for additional funds as a result of over-spending his allowance.

✔ The whole issue of money can be very sensitive, especially for families with limited financial resources. Students who are unable to participate in senior year activities that their peers take for granted may need help in dealing with feelings of isolation or alienation. Although it may be tempting to stretch family resources to enable your student to participate on the same terms as their classmates, it sends the wrong message about financial responsibility. Encourage them to be realistic about expenses that are outside of the family budget. You can help your student come up with ideas to earn extra money to cover some of the more important activities or identify lower cost alternatives (e.g. doing an internship in a field of interest instead of taking an expensive Spring Break trip). You should also try to enlist school administrators in identifying and promoting activities that would be more inclusive.

NOTES

_____

_____

_____

_____

_____

_____

_____

_____

_____

Out of the Starting Gate:

THE FALL SEMESTER

SEPTEMBER

CREATE A MASTER CALENDAR

✔ The first thing you need to do is get a handle on all the key dates and obligations so that you won't be playing "catch up" all year. Do not assume that your student will automatically provide what you need—information has a mysterious way of disappearing between school and home. Here are a few contacts for you to make as soon as school begins in the fall:

- Call the school administrative office and ask for a calendar. This is a great source for information on things like exam schedules and graduation-related activities.

- Call the academic advisor's office and ask for a schedule of key dates. This is an important source of information on when your student needs to submit their college applications and requests for recommendations. Academic advisors can also provide information about SAT/ACT testing dates and locations.

- The larger the school, the more important it is that students adhere strictly to the process and timing that is outlined. Advisors often have many students to support and it may not be possible for them to grant exceptions. In all cases, students should try and submit their information at the earliest date possible.

- Contact the yearbook advisor to find out when photographs need to be submitted. It is important to ask what size and format (black & white or color) the pictures should be in.

- Contact the faculty advisors for any extracurricular activities your child participates in for schedules (including post-season banquets, etc.).

✔ Once you have all this information, make up a Master Calendar that will help you stay on top of things. Review the calendar frequently with your student to ensure that no important dates are missed. It is especially important to be alert during the 1st semester, when there are many critical deadlines to be met (including college applications).

✔ This calendar is also important in helping you identify periods when your student can make college visits, which can be difficult to schedule with all that is going on in the fall. In making arrangements for these visits, your student will need to conform to their school's policy on excused absences. As a practical matter, you may want to defer visits until your student has been accepted and has narrowed their choices to a reasonable number. Campus visits can then be scheduled during the spring semester, when there is less somewhat less pressure.

SET UP A "CLUTTER CONTROL SYSTEM"

✔ You'll need to set up a system to handle the paper overload that happens during senior year. In addition to the mail that your student receives from colleges, they will also find themselves on the mailing lists of numerous vendors of graduation-related merchandise and services (e.g. photographers, T-shirt vendors, jewelers, party planners, travel agencies, formal wear rental shops, etc.) Here are two ideas that worked for us:

- Use a large box or crate as a catch-all for your student's mail. Put everything in this box as it comes in. Go through it once a week—preferably with your student—and sort items as follows: immediate action; file for later action; throw away.

> **Hint**: If your student has already made some decisions about colleges, you can get rid of a lot of the unwanted mail before it ever enters the house. For example, our son was certain that he wanted to attend school in the South or Southeast—so we could immediately "toss" all the mail that came from schools in other parts of the country.

- Use a letter-size file box for items that will be needed during the year. Make folders for each of your student's activities, as well as each of the colleges they apply to. Put all information regarding those subjects (flyers, notices, etc.) in their respective folders. That way the information will be easily accessible when needed.

ORGANIZE FOR THE COLLEGE ADMISSIONS PROCESS

✔ If your student has not finalized their list of college choices, it is important for them to meet with their academic advisor ASAP to discuss realistic options based on their interests and abilities. Once they've made their decisions, have your student contact the colleges to request an application packet. They should also ask for scholarship and/or financial aid information, if needed. Many colleges now allow students to request this information on-line. Find out if any of the schools on your student's list accept the Common Application (usually available through the school library or guidance office).

> **Hint**: If your student intends to file an Early Decision application, the entire process is greatly accelerated and you will need to govern yourselves accordingly. The decision to apply early should not be made lightly because it requires that a stu-

dent commit to attend the selected school if they are accepted. You should definitely consult with your student's academic advisor before deciding to go this route. Call to make an appointment as soon as school starts in the fall.

✔ If you have concerns about your student's academic performance or test scores, you may wish to schedule a special meeting with their academic advisor to discuss college choices and potential application strategies. Some families in this situation have found it helpful to work with a private consultant, who can spend the necessary time evaluating opportunities for their student. Parents of previous graduates and the school's guidance office can be good sources of recommendations.

✔ Be sure that you and your student understand the requirements for graduation and that they are registered for all of the courses necessary to meet these requirements. You should also check to see if your student's class schedule reflects an appropriate level of difficulty for the type of college that they are applying to (e.g. students applying to highly competitive colleges should definitely consider adding Advanced Placement courses to their schedule). Discuss this with your student's academic advisor if you have any questions.

✔ Many schools communicate college-related information at a special "Senior Night" program put on by the academic advisory office. During the program, the advisors may distribute copies of your student's most recent transcript, discuss graduation requirements, talk about the college admissions process in some detail, and provide testing and financial aid information. You can get many of your questions answered at this forum, so you should make every effort to attend along with your student. Contact the school early in the year to find out if they offer this type of program and put the date on your Master Calendar.

✔ Students must sign up for October SAT/ACT exams by mid-September (due dates are usually available from your student's academic advisor or college placement office). Information about the SAT test is also available on-line at the College Board website (www.collegeboard.org). The website address for information about the ACT test is www.act.org.

> **Hint**: Check to see if your school or local community organizations offer any SAT or ACT preparation classes during the weeks leading up to the test(s). These classes are usually given free of charge and can be a good supplement to individual preparation by your student. There are also a number of excellent computerized test preparation programs available. Some of these may be available through your school or public library.

✔ Have your student check with their academic advisor for information on scholarships and campus visits by college admissions representatives. Carefully check the deadline dates for sign-up and/or submitting required information and add those to your Master Calendar.

CAPTURE SENIOR YEAR MEMORIES

✔ Keeping an ongoing memory file is great way to capture all of the wonderful events and experiences that are part of your student's senior year. You can enlist your student's participation by stocking up on a supply of disposable cameras so they can take candid pictures of their friends and activities throughout the year. Encourage them to capture all of the "highlights" on film: first day of school, athletic events, Homecoming, dances, school plays, senior recognition events, etc. Remind them to bring home programs and other memorabilia that can serve as reminders of this special time in their lives. When in doubt, save everything! You can always sort it out later.

> **Hint**: There are many creative scrapbooking resources available that can help you turn these items into a wonderful keepsake. Consult magazines such as *Memory Makers* and *Creating Keepsakes* (both available on newsstands) for creative ideas, products and sources for purchasing supplies. Check their website addresses for subscription information at www.memorymakers.com or www.creatingkeepsakes.com.

GET INVOLVED

✔ There are many opportunities for parent involvement during senior year. Examples include: chaperoning at dances and class trips, planning and decorating for special events (team banquets, senior party, etc.), and contributing photographs or videos for year-end celebrations. There will likely be a special meeting of senior parents at which these and other opportunities will be identified and you will be asked to sign-up. If you do not receive a notice of such a meeting by mid-September, contact the school office or Parents Association president.

✔ Although your student may not seem thrilled at the idea of having you participate, you will find out later that your efforts to make their senior year special meant a lot to them. Even if you do not have a lot of extra time, make every effort to contribute in some way—perhaps by using a special talent. For example, I made photo collages for my son's football coaches and senior teammates that were presented at the annual awards banquet. Even though Jason had often made fun of my "obsession" with scrapbooking, he was very pleased that I had taken the time to create memorable gifts for his team.

ADDITIONAL IDEAS

✔ If your student is a visual artist, have slides professionally taken of their best 15-20 pieces of artwork completed during high school. Have the student ask their art teacher to help with the selection process. Slides should be sent along with applications to the colleges of their choice, following instructions provided on submitting samples of the student's work.

✔ Check out end of month clearance sales for markdowns on small dormitory items (e.g. message boards, etc.) that can be easily stored for next fall. Discounts can be 40%–50% off the original price.

NOTES

_____

_____

_____

_____

_____

_____

_____

_____

_____

_____

TAKE COLLEGE PLACEMENT EXAMS

✔ Many students first take the SAT and ACT tests in the spring of their junior year and retake the exams in October in an attempt to achieve a higher score. They are not penalized for doing this, since colleges will always accept the highest score that the student has achieved, with each part of the exam counted separately.

✔ Students have additional opportunities to take the SAT I & II exams in November and December. Registration for the November tests is usually completed in early October. (Dates can be obtained from your student's academic advisor or from the College Board and ACT websites).

LIST KEY DATES FOR COLLEGE ADMISSIONS

✔ Review the college application packets with your student and put critical dates on the Master Calendar. Completing the applications takes a good deal of time and thought. The more schools your student applies to, the more time they will need to budget to get everything submitted before the deadline dates.

✔ A number of colleges have December and early January deadlines, which tend to overlap with final exams and holiday activities. This is a good reason not to put everything off until the last minute. If your student gets started early, he or she will be able to put more effort into developing an application that best reflects their interests and abilities.

REQUEST RECOMMENDATIONS

✔ Have your student identify the teachers and other individuals who they will ask for recommendations. Then have them check with each person ahead of time to see if they are comfortable with providing a reference. The student should write a letter to the person that clearly indicates the date by which the recommendation is needed. To be on the safe side, ask for the recommendation to be sent a couple of weeks before the school's application deadline. The required recommendation form (with all appropriate information filled in), along with a pre-addressed stamped envelope should be included with your student's cover letter.

> **Hint**: Remember, popular teachers get asked to provide a lot of recommendations, so the earlier your student gets their request in, the better. Students in larger high schools should probably take care of this in September.

✔ When the student requests that someone provide a recommendation, it is important to supply that person with as much information as possible to help them write a convincing reference. A summary of the student's interests and activities would be helpful, as well as a statement about their career interests and reasons for wanting to attend a particular college. The student should always remember to thank the person providing the reference for their assistance in the admissions process. The time spent doing this can really pay off, as shown in the following example provided by the mother of one of my son's classmates:

> "Our son asked our pastor for a recommendation for a private college with which he had very close ties. Our church has 2000 members, and although Rev. Smith knew 'Bill' through his religious and church camp activities, he was less familiar with other aspects of his life. 'Bill' compiled a packet that included a copy of his completed application, his essay, a picture collage, an activity grid for the past four years, and a personal thank you note. The next week he received a note from Rev. Smith

stating that in all the years he had been writing recommendations he had never before received such helpful information. He went on to say that 'Bill' was obviously a conscientious, thorough and organized individual and he was sure that he would do well in college. A few days later, the school's director of admissions called 'Bill' and scheduled a time for a personal interview. He was accepted shortly thereafter."

BEGIN WORKING ON THE APPLICATION ESSAY

✔ Have your student get started on their application essay(s). Most colleges require at least one essay on a general topic, but some of the more selective colleges ask for more. To minimize the stress associated with the essay writing and revisions process, consider having your student work with another adult with whom they have a good rapport. They are more likely to accept constructive criticism and do the work necessary to "polish" their essay when a parent is not directly involved. Do offer to assist with typing or proofreading their final essay.

RESEARCH SCHOLARSHIP AND FINANCIAL AID OPPORTUNITIES

✔ There are many resources available to assist students and their parents in identifying money to pay for college. Your high school or public library is a good place to start, since it will have a number of publications on hand that list financial aid sources. College financial aid offices can also provide information on government grants and loans, as well as private scholarships only available to students attending that particular school. A wealth of information can also be found on the Web. See page 68 for a listing of reference materials concerning financial aid for college.

✔ To receive any type of federal financial aid, you must complete the Free Application for Federal Student Aid (FAFSA) form. This form is usually available through your student's school, and can also be obtained from the U.S. Department of Education at 1-800-433-3243 or www.ed.gov. The earliest date that the FAFSA form can be filed is January 1. To have the best chance of receiving aid, you should plan to file as soon as possible after January 1.

✔ Be sure to submit scholarship applications according to the published deadlines. Some private scholarship sources require that applications be submitted in the Fall.

> **Hint:** Keep copies of all completed application materials in your reference file, noting the dates on which they were submitted. Just to be on the safe side, you may also wish to request confirmation of delivery from the post office in order to have proof that your application was received by the deadline.

ADDITIONAL IDEAS

✔ Work with your student to prepare two helpful attachments to be submitted along with their college applications. These attachments can help provide admissions committees with a better understanding of the unique contribution your student would be able to make to their college community:

Activity Grid: A 1-page summary of their key activities, including school involvements, volunteer work, part-time and summer employment. For each activity, include the years of participation (Grades 9–12), the time spent (hours/week, weeks/year), and offices held, honors or awards. The heading should include the student's name and Social Security number. A sample activity grid is provided on page 71.

Photo Collage: Select 15-20 pictures that show your student in a variety of situations that reflect their interests and personality. Be sure to include at least one "head shot." Mount the pictures on a 16 x 20 posterboard using rubber cement or other adhesive so that corners lie flat. Label the collage with your student's name and Social Security number, as well as captions that identify the situations illustrated in the photos. Lettering should be dark and large enough to be read when reduced by approx. 50%. Take the posterboard to a commercial photo finishing lab (look in the Yellow Pages) and ask for 8 x 10 prints. Call ahead to find out the processing time to ensure that the prints will be available when you plan to mail your applications.

NOTES

_____

_____

_____

_____

_____

_____

_____

_____

_____

NOVEMBER

GET SERIOUS ABOUT COLLEGE APPLICATIONS

✔ This is the time for your student to really get down to the business of completing those college applications. Review the deadline dates. Be sure that your student schedules time to work on completing the final essays and application forms. Also check to see if they have contacted teachers for recommendations.

> **Hint**: Even if your student has filed an Early Decision application, they should prepare applications for several other schools just in case. These applications should not have to be mailed until after the Early Decision notification date.

✔ Students should also re-take the SAT and/or ACT exams, if needed, to improve their score. Registration for the December test dates is usually completed in early November.

✔ Review mid-semester grades with your student and identify areas for improvement. Remind them that 1st semester senior year grades can be an important factor in the admissions process—especially if they show a positive trend.

ADVANCE PLANNING FOR SPRING BREAK

✔ Spring Break is an excellent time to visit college campuses. Check with the admissions office to find out if school will be in session during the time your student is on vacation. If so, you can inquire about what opportunities would be available for your student to learn more about the college during their visit (e.g. campus tours, class attendance, meetings with deans and faculty, overnight stay in a dormitory, etc.). You may even be able to schedule visits to several schools over the vacation period. Be sure to make transportation and hotel arrangements well in advance, since school vacations tend to be peak travel periods.

✔ Another possibility offered with some frequency is a trip abroad that is connected with academic coursework or extracurricular activities. If your student is interested in participating in this type of trip, be sure to understand the costs involved as well as the arrangements that have been made for supervision of the students during their visit. You will also need to discuss the financial arrangements with your student, including any contributions they will be expected to make.

> **Hint**: Students sometimes work together to raise funds for their trip through activities such as car washes, candy sales, etc. Volunteering to organize the fundraising effort is another great opportunity for parental involvement.

✔ It has also become popular at some high schools for students to plan an unchaperoned (or minimally chaperoned) Spring Break trip during senior year. Mexico—where drinking is legal at age 16—is one popular destination. If you are not OK with this, you'll want to make it clear to your student well ahead of time.

What worked for us was to plan a vacation with several other families, so our son could be with friends and not feel he was missing out on all the fun. The kids roomed and participated in many activities together, getting together with the parents for morning and evening meals. They had a great time, but the presence of parents kept a rein on undesirable behaviors. If you present your student with an acceptable alternative early in the year, it can cut down on the nagging and pleading later on.

✔ If travel is not an option, encourage your student to explore possible internship opportunities in their field of interest. Potential sources of information include teachers, school counselors, relatives, family friends, and directories of internship opportunities (available in libraries or on the Web).

> **Hint**: Successful internships can lead to opportunities for paid summer or part-time employment, so remind your student to always put their best foot forward.

NOTES

_____

_____

_____

_____

_____

_____

_____

_____

_____

_____

COMPLETE
COLLEGE APPLICATIONS

✔ Have your student try to get all their applications submitted before Christmas break. It is such a relief to get this out of the way so they can really enjoy the holidays. Remember to check that all appropriate forms and fees are included along with the neatly typed application form. Follow mailing instructions exactly.

✔ Last chance for students to re-take SAT/ACT exams before applications are due.

✔ Complete the FAFSA form and other financial aid applications that may be required by the schools that your student is applying to.

EARLY DECISION/EARLY ACTION NOTIFICATION

✔ Early Decision/Early Action letters arrive between December 1 and December 15. For students who are accepted at the school of their choice, this can provide a great sense of relief. It can also bring on a premature case of "Senioritis"—a drop in motivation caused by a sense that high school is completed.

> **Hint**: While celebrating your student's success in gaining admission, you also need to remind them that "it ain't over 'til it's over." If they read the fine print on their acceptance letter, they will find that their admission is contingent on continuing a high level of performance.

✔ Students who are not accepted in this round often face tremendous disappointment because they have invested a great deal in the decision. It is very painful to be told that your first choice school does not reciprocate your interest. Parents of these students need to help them re-focus their attention on completing the application process for their alternative schools. It is also important to remind them that they have an opportunity to re-apply to their first choice school after successfully completing a year or two at another school. Acceptance rates for transfer students are much higher than those for incoming freshmen—even at the most selective colleges.

COMPILE AN ADDRESS LIST FOR GRADUATION ANNOUNCEMENTS

✔ Start putting together a list of the names and addresses of people to whom you will be sending graduation announcements. This job may be easier if done when you are addressing your holiday cards. Also, be sure to note any change of address information that is included in the greeting cards that you receive from friends and relatives.

✔ It is not too early to begin informing relatives and friends of the schedule for graduation activities. If you have a number of guests coming from out of town, it would be a good idea to provide information on hotels that would be convenient. If you are planning an Open House or party at the time of graduation, that information should also be included.

EMPHASIZE FAMILY TIME

✔ Despite the hectic pace of the holidays, try to carve out some special time to spend together as a family. This is likely to be the last year that your student will be a full-time member of your household, so it is important to make the most of your time together. Remember that next year you'll be welcoming home a young adult who will probably spend much of their holiday challenging the relevance of house rules and running out the door to visit friends.

> **Hint**: Sit down with your student and a calendar to agree on "family time" and free time when they can schedule separate activities. Listen to their needs, but be firm about those family events that are non-negotiable (e.g. Christmas Eve dinner at Grandma's).

NOTES

_____

_____

_____

_____

_____

_____

_____

_____

Into the Home Stretch:

THE SPRING SEMESTER

JANUARY

MAINTAIN ACADEMIC FOCUS

✔ Review your student's 1st semester grades and 2nd semester schedule to be sure they are on track for completing graduation requirements. You should also check to see if your student is maintaining the level of academic difficulty that would be expected by the schools to which they have applied. It is never a good idea to give the appearance that the student took a "holiday" from academic pursuits once their college applications were completed.

✔ If you have any concerns about your student's academic performance, do not rely on their word that "everything is OK." Make an appointment to discuss your questions with your student's academic advisor. Request *written confirmation* of how any discrepancies (e.g. disputed grades, incompletes, etc.) have been resolved.

GET A JUMP ON GRADUATION PLANNING

✔ Finalize the date for your student's graduation party or Open House. If you are planning to hold the event away from home, you'll want to make reservations because many popular locations (e.g. park pavilions, recreation centers, etc.) get booked up quickly. If possible, coordinate with the parents of your child's special friends so that their celebrations will not be held at exactly the same time. If your student would like to have a joint celebration with friends, contact the parents to be sure that you have similar expectations regarding the type and cost of the party. If this is not the case, you will have plenty of time to plan a separate event.

> **Hint**: If you do not have guests coming from out-of-town, you may wish to schedule your celebration at a time other than graduation week. Several of our son's friends had their parties later in the summer—when there were no other conflicting events—and had excellent attendance.

✔ Start organizing photos and other memorabilia to display during graduation festivities. This is a wonderful way to let people know about your student's personality and accomplishments. Select favorite pictures from different stages of your child's life—particularly those that show them with special friends or involved in favorite activities. Be sure to feature any special talents or interests, along with academic or extracurricular honors (e.g. trophies, medals, certificates, etc.).

✔ If you are contemplating a big project, such as a scrapbook or memory quilt, be sure to allow enough time for it to be completed. You may also wish to attend a class to enhance your skills or provide creative ideas for your project. Classes are often available through community education programs or retailers of craft supplies.

NOTES

_____

_____

_____

_____

_____

_____

PLAYING THE WAITING GAME

✔ Schools with rolling admissions policies often start sending acceptance/rejection letters beginning in February. It can be hard for students when their friends begin getting good news and their status is still in limbo. It can be harder still if the first news that they hear is a rejection. As a parent, you need to help your child cope with the emotional swings that occur as part of this process. (See the tips for December under Early Decision/Early Admission).

✔ Begin a dialog with your student to help them determine the criteria they will use to make their final college decision. Encourage them to put together a chart comparing the various colleges on the factors that they consider to be most important.

✔ Visit college campuses as time permits.

SPRUCING THINGS UP AROUND THE HOUSE

✔ Make a list of any household projects (e.g. landscaping, painting, floor refinishing, etc.) that need to be completed prior to graduation, and develop a timeline for getting these tasks done. If you plan to hire someone else to do the work, you'll want to get on their schedule as soon as possible to avoid last minute disappointment.

NOTES

_____

_____

_____

NOTES

MARCH

The Waiting Game Continues

✔ Look for additional admissions decision letters.

✔ Carry out Spring Break plans.

✔ Be prepared for a major outbreak of "Senioritis" after Spring Break. Even the most dedicated students can suffer a loss of motivation when they start to see the "finish line." Stay alert for any drastic changes in study habits or attendance that might actually jeopardize their graduation status.

Graduation Planning

✔ Call the school office to get the final schedule of graduation events. Inform out-of-town guests of starting times for key events so they can adjust travel arrangements, if necessary. If your student plays a spring sport, be sure to check the schedule for any games or tournaments that may conflict with graduation-related activities. This occurs more frequently than you might imagine. When Jason was a senior, the state baseball tournament finals were scheduled on the same date as graduation ceremonies for most of the public and private schools in the area! When notified of the conflict, school administrators pushed back the starting time of the graduation ceremony so that our seniors could participate in the tournament. If you note any issues of this type, bring them to the attention of coaches and school administrators as soon as possible.

✔ Start to look for information about ordering announcements, caps & gowns, and other graduation paraphernalia. Some high schools mail this information directly to the home, but many just send it via the students. The timing for ordering varies greatly, depending on when graduations are typically held in your area. Call the school office to check dates if you have not received an order form by Spring Break. Be sure to give some thought to the number of announcements you plan to send out so they can all be ordered at the same time. It will generally be more expensive if you have to go back and order additional announcements.

Hint: You may be able to order graduation party or Open House invitations from the same company that provides the announcements. If this option is not available, you will want to order invitations from another source, or design your own. When ordering invitations, keep in mind that you will need to mail them at least 3 weeks prior to the event.

NOTES

_____

_____

_____

_____

_____

_____

_____

_____

_____

THE WAIT IS OVER

✔ All admissions decision letters should be received by April 15th. If your student does not hear from any of their colleges by this date, they should immediately contact the admissions office to determine the status of their application. If necessary, they should contact their academic advisor for assistance.

✔ If your student has been accepted at any schools that they have definitely decided NOT to attend, have them promptly send a letter expressing their thanks and indicating their intention to matriculate elsewhere. This will enable the school to fill the slot with another student from their waiting list.

✔ Your student should also begin to receive information about scholarships and financial aid around this time. Read the materials carefully, so that you can evaluate the offers your student receives from various schools. In comparing offers, give greater weight to those that contain a higher percentage of grants and scholarships (money that does not have to be repaid). Pay close attention to response dates and any additional data that you and/or your student need to provide in order to confirm that the funds will be available for the fall semester.

> **Hint**: If the financial aid awarded by your student's first choice school is insufficient, you may be able to negotiate an increase by providing additional information about family circumstances or advising them of higher offers from other schools. You may have additional leverage if your student falls in the highly desirable category (e.g. top grades, high scores on the SAT/ACT, unique talents or fills a particular need for the school). Check out the financial aid resources listed in the

Appendix for suggestions on how to negotiate a financial aid offer.

✔ Offers of admission and/or financial aid are sometimes contingent on your student completing certain courses or attending a summer program sponsored by the college. Students who receive athletic scholarships may also be required to attend special camps over the summer. Be sure that your student is willing and able to comply with the requirements that are outlined before making their final decision about which school to attend.

✔ Be sure that your student notifies the school of their choice before the May 1st candidate reply deadline. Follow the instructions received along with your student's letter of acceptance in terms of sending a deposit and other required forms.

GETTING READY FOR PROMS AND PARTIES

✔ If your son will be attending the senior prom, you'll want to reserve his tuxedo by mid-April. Some of the more popular styles are booked quickly and selection can be very limited if they wait until a few weeks before the event. The same holds true if they plan to reserve a limousine. Be sure to make these arrangements at least four weeks in advance. Allow more time if there are several schools in your area holding proms on the same evening.

✔ Although girls do not have to be concerned about reserving formal attire, my sources tell me that it is not unusual for it to take three to four weeks to find just the 'right' dress for a special occasion. You'll also want to allow time for alterations, which are often necessary on a formal gown.

✔ Be sure to have your student check out the many prom-related websites for ideas on prom attire, beauty tips, corsages, limousine rentals, dining out, photos, etc. Some of the more popular sites include: YourProm (www.yourprom.com), Prom Night (www.prom-night.com), and the Prom Planning Network (www.proms.net). Purchasing prom dresses on-line is still a relatively new phenomenon, but it's worth taking a look at sites like Simply Dresses.com (www.simplydresses.com) for shopping ideas.

✔ It has become increasingly common for a committee of parents to plan an all-night party following the graduation ceremony that is attended by the entire senior class. This type of organized activity solves a lot of problems and helps ensure that students have fun in a safe environment. If nothing like this has been planned at your school, you may wish to get together with the parents of your child's close friends and plan something on a smaller scale. The keys to making this work are to have the parents agree on a common set of rules for the evening (e.g. no liquor or drug use) and to provide adequate supervision.

✔ If your student will not be attending an organized post-graduation event, you'll need to spend some time discussing their plans to ensure that they meet with your approval. At a minimum, you'll want to know where they plan to go and with whom, transportation arrangements, and who will cover the costs. You will also need to agree on an acceptable time for them to come home. In these situations, it is reasonable to allow some extension of the normal curfew—but it is generally not a good idea to allow them to stay out all night without adult supervision.

NOTES

_____

_____

_____

_____

_____

_____

ACADEMIC WRAP-UP

✔ If your student is required to send a final transcript of their grades to the college of their choice, request that their academic advisor send it as soon as 2nd semester grades are available. Many schools have a special form for this purpose.

✔ Be sure that your student completes and turns in any year-end projects that may be due. They also need to schedule adequate time to study for final exams.

✔ If there are any outstanding issues concerning your student's grades or graduation status, have your student meet with their academic advisor early in the month to confirm that they have been resolved. You should personally follow-up with the school concerning any issues that have not been addressed to your satisfaction.

> **Hint**: Many schools schedule special year-end programs in early May, in order to avoid the rush surrounding graduation. These programs often provide opportunities for recognition of individual graduates, and can be very moving. Take your camera and plenty of Kleenex!

FINALIZE DETAILS FOR YOUR PARTY OR OPEN HOUSE

✔ If you are hosting a party, talk to your student about your expectations (e.g. budget, number of people to be invited, whether guests will be allowed to bring dates who do not attend their school, hours of the party, food, adult supervision, etc.). Be sure to discuss any rules guests will be expected to follow and remind your student that you will not allow liquor to be served—even if some of the guests might be of legal drinking age. As the host of the party, you can be subject to significant legal consequences if one of your underage guests is later involved in an accident while under the influence of alcohol.

> **Hint**: Gatecrashers can be a problem. It is important to have enough adult chaperones (including several males) to discourage uninvited guests from attempting to get into the party. Try to enlist parents of your student's friends to assist you with the chaperoning duties.

✔ If you are hosting a party or open house that will include relatives and friends of the family, it is a good idea to have a conversation with your student about what you will expect of them during the event. Since their priority is likely to be spending time with their friends, it is important for them to understand their role as guest of honor (e.g. personally greeting all attendees, making pleasant conversation, circulating through the room, posing for pictures, etc.).

✔ If your party is being held during the height of the graduation "season," there are likely to be a number of other parties being held on the same day. Be sure to discuss the specific hours that your student must be present at the event being held in their honor. For example, our son's open house was held from 2 PM–5 PM on the Saturday following graduation. We agreed that he must be at home between the hours of 1:30 PM and 5:30 PM, which allowed him to attend other open houses both before and after his own.

✔ Mail graduation announcements and party/open house invitations to arrive at least 3 weeks prior to the event. 4–6 weeks is preferable if the event is being held at a location that requires confirmation of the number of guests attending.

✔ Finalize and confirm all arrangements (reservations, catering arrangements, equipment rentals, entertainment, etc.)

✔ Complete major projects for display during graduation festivities. Collect other memorabilia in one location, frame photographs, etc.

> **Hint**: Consider involving younger siblings in putting together a scrapbook or display for your graduating senior. Their work can be acknowledged during the party.

DRESSING THE PART

✔ If your school has specific requirements for graduation attire (e.g. what is to be worn with or under your student's cap and gown) consider yourself lucky. When this decision is left open, you will find a wide range in what students consider acceptable to wear. Bare feet, underwear, signs supporting various causes, and painted faces are only a few of the choices students have "modeled" at graduation ceremonies. There are also persistent rumors about one or more students going au naturel under their gowns. While a number of parents consider this disrespectful, there are others who have no problem with whatever choice their student makes.

> **Hint**: If it is important to you that your student present a more traditional appearance (e.g. dress or skirt for girls; suit or sport coat for guys), then discuss it with them in advance. At the same time, you may also want to talk about what your student will wear at their graduation party or open house. An offer to purchase a new outfit can often do the trick in gaining their cooperation.

GIFTS—THE ART OF GIVING
AND RECEIVING

✔ Purchase graduation cards and/or gifts for other graduates you are planning to recognize. The etiquette surrounding gift-giving can be summarized as follows:

- Students typically do not exchange graduation gifts with each other, because they would go broke (significant others and friends of long-standing may be an exception). They will usually acknowledge special friends with a card containing a handwritten message.

- Parents generally acknowledge only those graduates who they know well. Without a doubt, the gift that is most appreciated is a check. $20–$25 is the norm, however, the amount can be higher depending on your budget and the closeness of the relationship. Other popular gifts include: pre-paid phone cards; gift certificates to national food chains like McDonald's, Burger King, KFC, Pizza Hut, etc. or clothing, sporting goods and electronic equipment stores; pre-paid gift cards to national chains such as Wal-Mart; K-Mart and Target; and T-shirts, sweatshirts, etc. with their college insignia. You can also check with the graduate's parents to see if they have any special requests.

✔ Talk to your student ahead of time about what will be done with the money that they receive as graduation gifts. If you do not do this, there is a great tendency for this money to "disappear" into their general cash flow and they will have little to show for it. In our case, we agreed that Jason would apply his graduation money towards the purchase of a personal computer to use at college. He was free to use any leftover funds for other college-related expenses (e.g. items for his dorm room, clothing, books, etc.).

✔ Have your student keep a running list of all graduation gifts they receive and acknowledge them promptly with a note. Purchase stationery and stamps ahead of time, so there will be no reason for them to procrastinate. All thank you notes should be mailed before the student leaves for college.

> **Hint**: Although a handwritten note is preferred, many students use their computer skills to generate attractive thank-you notes. At a minimum, each note should refer to the sender's specific gift and have a hand written signature.

MISCELLANEOUS DETAILS

✔ Select and order your child's graduation gift. Remember that monograms and other personalization take additional time, so get those orders in early.

✔ Be sure that your cameras are in top working condition. Put new batteries in your still camera and charge your video batteries. Take a test roll of film with each camera you plan to use so that you can correct any problems before the "big day."

✔ Confirm travel and housing arrangements for out-of-town guests. Make arrangements for airport pick-up or transportation to graduation events, if necessary.

NOTES

_____

_____

_____

_____

_____

_____

_____

The Grand Finale:

CEREMONIES AND CELEBRATIONS

GRADUATION DAY

✔ Try to keep the day as stress-free as possible. Avoid over-scheduling and last minute additions to your "to do" list. Let other family members share responsibility for graduation day tasks, but put as little pressure as possible on the graduate.

✔ It is a good idea to eat before going to the graduation ceremony. If you decide to eat out, be sure to allow sufficient time for your meal and travel to the graduation site when making your reservations. If you decide to serve a meal at home, make it simple and let someone else take care of the cooking. Many supermarkets have catering services that offer a wide variety of menu items. Use paper plates and plastic forks so there's minimal clean-up.

✔ Make sure that your student has all of their graduation attire and that any items that need to be ironed (e.g. gowns) are wrinkle-free. If your student will be dressing at school, check to see that all necessary items are packed before they leave home.

✔ It is a good idea to take family photos before leaving for the graduation ceremony. That way you can be sure that you won't miss any critical shots.

✔ Plan to arrive at the location for the graduation ceremony well ahead of time so that you can get a good seat. Seating is generally on a "first come, first served" basis, and you do not want to find yourself stuck in a poor location.

> **Hint**: Agree with your student on a place that you will meet following the ceremony, so that friends and family can assemble for greetings and more picture-taking. There is nothing more frustrating than trying to locate each other in a large crowd.

✔ If your student will be attending a party following the graduation ceremony, be sure that you have detailed information about where they will be and who they will be with. Before they leave, you'll want to confirm your expectations about appropriate behavior and when they are expected to be home.

> **Hint**: If you have a cell phone, lend it to your student for the evening so they will have no difficulty in contacting you in the event of an emergency or other unexpected developments that might occur. At a minimum, be sure that they have change or a credit card number to call home if necessary.

THE DAY OF YOUR GRADUATION PARTY OR OPEN HOUSE

✔ As with the day of graduation, you'll want to keep stress at a minimum. Get all family members involved in last minute tasks (e.g. decorations, food pick-up, putting up directional signs, etc.)

✔ Be sure to assign a responsible person to take pictures throughout your event. Although they do not have to be a professional, it should be someone who has demonstrated some skill with photography in the past. You should be sure that this person understands how to work your camera and has plenty of film to capture your special celebration.

> **Hint**: You may also wish to equip your photographer with a list of specific pictures that you would like taken (e.g. the graduate with his parents and grandparents, etc.).

✔ Remind the guest of honor about their hosting duties.

✔ Relax and have fun. After all of the planning and hard work involved in getting to this point, you deserve to enjoy the festivities.

NOTES

_____

_____

_____

_____

_____

_____

_____

_____

_____

_____

_____

_____

_____

_____

NOTES

_____

_____

_____

_____

_____

_____

_____

_____

_____

_____

_____

_____

_____

_____

_____

_____

_____

_____

_____

_____

_____

_____

Transitioning:

THE SUMMER AFTER THE SENIOR YEAR

LATE JUNE-JULY

COMMUNICATIONS FROM THE COLLEGE

✔ First semester tuition payments and room deposits are typically due sometime in late June or early July. Be alert for communications from your student's college concerning these matters. Review the billing statement carefully, and be sure to adhere to the schedule for submitting your payments. Tuition bills should reflect any financial aid that has been awarded to your student by the school. Contact the financial aid office immediately if you have any questions after comparing the billing statement to your student's award letter.

> **Hint**: Make sure to keep a record of all payments made to the college, as well as any cancelled checks. This can be important in the event that there is ever a dispute concerning your student's account.

✔ Once the room deposit is received, your student will be assigned to a dormitory. Some schools communicate roommate assignments at the same time the student is notified of their dormitory placement. If your student receives this information, encourage him/her to contact their prospective roommate as soon as possible. Even if distance does not allow your student to meet his/her room-mate in person before school begins, they can start to get acquainted through letters, e-mail or telephone calls. Topics to discuss include sleeping and study habits, interests, likes and dislikes, etc. They can also review the list of items that the school suggests they bring and decide if there are things they can share instead of having duplicates.

> **Hint:** If you do not want to be considered hope-lessly outdated and uncool, do not suggest that your student talk to his/her roommate about coor-dinating room décor. When I did this, Jason was horrified that I would suggest such a thing—a feel-ing that was shared by his friends, both male and female. Although giving up your vision of a room with matching bedspreads and curtains may be hard, the reality is that most dorm rooms are so messy that you can't really tell what the décor is anyway.

✔ By mid-July, you should also have received information about freshman orientation and registration. Be aware that you may need to send in a separate deposit for the orientation. You should also know that many colleges (especially those in the South) hold freshman orientation programs before Labor Day, which creates an abbreviated summer for students attending those schools. In order to avoid conflict with the time that your student is expected to arrive at orientation, you'll want to check the school calendar before planning family activities.

✔ Decide how your student will travel to school and make travel reservations as soon as possible after receiving information about when they are required to be on cam-pus. If other family members will be accompanying your student to college, you will also need to make arrange-ments for their transportation and lodging at the same time. Remember that hotels in college towns tend to fill up quickly during the peak season.

> **Hint**: As a rule of thumb, parents should plan to stay around campus just long enough to get their student moved in, ensure that his or her student accounts are in order, establish a banking relationship and get the telephone and computer hooked up. These activities should take no longer than 2-3 days.

✔ Most colleges will require evidence that your student is in good health. A medical form will likely be included along with the information on registration. You will need to have this form signed by a physician and submitted to the school before your student can attend classes. If your student has not had a recent physical exam, you'll want to make an appointment early in the summer so that there won't be any problems getting the medical form completed in time to meet the school's deadline.

Although colleges do not typically request information concerning your student's dental health, you will also want to be sure that their teeth and gums are in good condition. Make an appointment for a dental check up early in the summer, so that any cavities or other problems can be taken care of before your student leaves for college.

> **Hint**: If your student has any medical or dental conditions that will require treatment while they are away at school, you should discuss this with the student health service at the college and seek their assistance in identifying appropriate medical resources in the local area. You should also ask your family physician for complete records regarding your student's diagnosis and treatment history. They should also be willing to speak with the medical personnel who will be involved in your student's treatment while at college.

MONEY MATTERS

✔ Help your student put together a budget for their college expenses. They should first list all sources of income they can draw upon during the school year (e.g. family savings, financial aid awards, allowance, earnings from part-time or summer jobs, work-study positions, etc.). They should then list all of the expenses that will need to be covered by these funds. The balance remaining after paying for tuition, room and board, and books is what they will have left to cover discretionary expenses.

✔ Discretionary expenses cover a very broad range—things like telephone bills, extra food, clothing, entertainment, trips home, personal care and grooming, laundry, etc. Parents will need to make their own determination about how much they are willing and able to contribute towards these expenses. In the interest of encouraging financial responsibility in your student, I strongly encourage you to put some type of limit on your contributions—even if there is no economic need to do so. Most adults have to learn to live within a certain income, and it is not too soon for your student to begin acquiring this skill while in college.

✔ To get a better idea of what to budget for discretionary expenses, talk to other parents of college-age students about their experiences. We were fortunate to know a number of parents in similar circumstances, and quickly found that their supplemental contributions were within a $50 range. We used this as a benchmark for setting Jason's allowance, with a provision that we would make adjustments after first semester based on his actual experiences. Our goal was to provide him with enough money to cover all of his basic needs and some extras, but not so much that he could do everything he liked.

> **Hint**: Encourage your student to work during the summer and save a significant portion of their earnings, even if they do not have to contribute

towards major expenses like tuition, room and board. They can then draw on these savings during the school year for expenses that are not covered by their allowance. You will find that they will become much more discriminating about what is considered a "necessity" when they are required to use their own money.

CURFEWS AND HOUSE RULES

✔ Even if you had relatively few problems with curfews and house rules during high school, there will likely be some challenges following graduation. There is something about going through this rite of passage that causes many students to feel that they have been immediately elevated to adult status—along with which comes the freedom to make all of their own choices. They may express these feelings verbally or by ignoring rules they had previously obeyed.

✔ Dealing with these issues can be very hard on the parent-child relationship. You may experience "flashbacks" to the early days of adolescence, when you both struggled with the growing pains associated with moving from one stage of development to another. Your student will be torn between anticipation of the freedom and new experiences that await them and a sense of losing the familiar patterns and relationships that anchored their childhood. As a parent, you will experience conflict between encouraging independent decision-making and providing the structure and discipline necessary for your student's continued development into a responsible adult.

✔ In the interest of maintaining family harmony during this period, it is a good idea to talk with your student about expectations. It may be helpful to have them articulate the specific areas in which they would like to have more freedom. You may be surprised that what they ask for is often less than you might have thought when they simply expressed blanket frustration with "being treated like a child." After listening to Jason complain about his "juvenile" curfew, we asked him what he thought was reasonable. To our surprise, the time that he named was only an hour later than his former curfew—a request we found easy to grant. The funny thing was that most of the time he came in earlier than the time we had agreed upon. He had the satisfaction of feeling like he was in control and we got to see that he could make appropriate decisions about when to come home, even when he had the freedom to stay out later.

✔ Of course, not all situations can be resolved that easily. However, unless a request negatively impacts the rights of other members of the family or is otherwise inconsistent with your family values, you should try to seek an area for compromise. By giving your student the ability to exercise greater decision-making authority while still within the family "safety net," you can have a greater sense of confidence that they will make good choices when they are on their own.

PREPARING TO LEAVE HOME

Sometime during the summer, your student will start making the emotional adjustment to the fact that they will shortly be entering college. Even if they will not be going far from home, they can experience intense feelings about the impending separation from family and friends. There is a wide range in how young people deal with these feelings, but there are some signs to look for:

✔ *Questioning their college decision:* Your student may demonstrate their anxiety by expressing last minute doubts about their choice of college. If the school they plan to attend is in a distant location, they may speculate that they would be better off staying at home and attending a local college. Some students even go so far as to suggest postponing college for a year or so—without having any well-thought out plan as to how they might productively spend their time. Faced with this situation, parents would be well advised to remain calm and supportive. At all costs, avoid statements that reinforce doubts that your student might have about their ability to cope. After the drama has subsided, you will have an opportunity to help them focus on the positive aspects of their choice.

> **Hint**: Reviewing the list of criteria that your student used to make their original decision can help remind them of the many reasons that the school they selected is a good "fit" given their interests and goals.

This may also be a good time to connect with other students from your area who will be attending the same school in the fall (other prospective freshmen or upperclassmen who may be at home for the summer). These introductions can help give your student a greater sense of security when they arrive on campus.

✔ *Clinging to High School Friends:* The prospect of losing the people who provide one of their primary sources of validation can be unsettling for many students. That is a key reason behind their desire to spend as much time as possible in the company of friends as the date for leaving home draws nearer. Without the pressures of studying or athletic activities during the week, every night becomes an opportunity for socializing. Jason and a group of his friends typically ended up at someone's home most summer evenings. There seemed to be no particular agenda for the time they spent together—just hanging out and having fun.

Parents need to recognize the importance of this activity in providing a reservoir of self-esteem for their student to draw upon before they establish friendships in their new surroundings. However, they may also need to set some limits about the amount of time devoted to social activities to ensure that their student is getting proper rest and fulfilling their family and employment obligations.

Encourage your student to host some of the gatherings, which will keep them at home more than otherwise might be the case.

Suggest that your student collect the e-mail addresses of their high school friends. We were surprised at how frequently Jason and his buddies kept in touch by using the "instant messenger" services that are available on-line. One enterprising young man even developed a website where members of the class could post news (like when they would be visiting home) and other contact information.

> **Hint**: Keep a supply of disposable cameras available and encourage your student to take candid pictures while hanging out with friends during the summer. When placed in a collage or small memory album, these pictures can be a source of comfort for the homesick college student.

✔ *Withdrawal from Family:* Rather than deal with the challenge of separating from family all at once, your student may start to distance themselves gradually over the summer. It is important for parents to recognize that this is a coping mechanism—not a rejection. You'll want to strike a balance between giving them the space they require to make the adjustment and fulfilling your own need to spend as much time as possible with them before they leave home.

One idea that has worked for several families we know is for each parent to make a regular "date" to spend time with their student doing something they both enjoy. The activity doesn't have to be elaborate, costly or time consuming; in fact the only requirement is that it provide an opportunity for 1:1 interaction. For example, Jason and I would regularly go out to breakfast on Saturday mornings, while he and my husband went on a weeklong fishing trip and attended several sporting events together. Having this time together allowed us to engage our son in conversation about important subjects in a relaxed, low-key atmosphere. It was also fun to have him all to ourselves—if only for a little while. These interactions made us much more accepting when he felt the need to create some distance.

Hint: If your student has other siblings at home, they would probably benefit from some 1:1 time also. If siblings are far apart in age or do not regularly spend much time with each other, you may want to be on the lookout for creative opportunities to bring them together, e.g. pairing them as roommates on a family vacation, etc.

NOTES

_____

_____

_____

_____

_____

_____

_____

_____

_____

_____

AUGUST–EARLY SEPTEMBER

PACKING BASICS

✔ Review the list of items that your student's college suggested that they bring with them to school. To expand your thinking about what your student will need, take a look at the college packing checklist on page 72.

✔ Once you and your student have agreed about what will be on their list, separate the items into two categories:

(1) *Things that can be easily acquired locally once your student arrives on campus.* This category typically includes inexpensive items such as toiletries, cosmetics, laundry and cleaning supplies, food, and school supplies. It may also include items that are available for rental through the school (e.g. small refrigerators). If there will be access to a car when your student arrives on campus, the number of items that can be purchased locally can be expanded to include things that are bulky (e.g. bedding, wastebaskets, etc.) and things that plug in (e.g. televisions, CD players, stereos/ speakers, telephones, small appliances, etc.). Since time is likely to be limited, you'll want to make a detailed shopping list and get good directions to the nearest discount stores.

> **Hint**: Although it is likely that you will want to purchase personal computers ahead of time, you may want to look into taking delivery after your student arrives on campus. If the computer was purchased at a national chain, perhaps you can arrange for it to be picked up at a store near the campus. If it was purchased on line, you should arrange for direct shipment rather than having it

> delivered to your home and transporting it your-self.

(2) **_Things that your student will bring from home._** Standard items in this category include clothing, jewelry, prescription medicines, specialized equipment for sports or hobbies, and personal memorabilia (photo albums, yearbooks, etc.). The list can also be expanded according to personal preference. To track progress, you'll want to make up a 3-column chart listing all of the items in this category in the first column. The second column will be used to check off when the item has been acquired, and the third column will be used to check off when the item has been packed. Post this chart in a prominent location so that it will always be "top of mind."

If you have room, it is a good idea to set up a "staging area" where you can begin to assemble all of the items that need to be packed. Having everything in one place will decrease the chances that something important will be left behind. The trick to using this approach is in the timing. You can't do it too far ahead because you will have difficulty keeping your student (and possibly other family members) from using the assembled items. When I tried organizing Jason's clothes a month ahead of time, I found that he kept wearing the T-shirts and underwear from the "take to college" pile because he didn't want his favorite items out of circulation that long. I'd recommend starting no more than a week to ten days before your student's departure date.

Don't forget to pack some reminders of home and family. You might want to include a prized possession or two, as well as photos of your student with family members and pets. Putting the pictures in a nice photo album or scrapbook, along with notes of encouragement from family and friends is a nice touch.

> **Hint:** If your student will be traveling by air, you will want to check the airline's policy and rates on extra baggage. It may be less expensive to ship some heavier items (e.g. trunks) ahead of time using another method of transportation.

IMPORTANT PAPERS

✔ Put together a file containing all of the important papers that your student should take with them to college. (Note: The expandable accordion folders with an elastic band are ideal for this purpose.) At a minimum, this file should include copies of the following documents:

- Letter of admission
- Cancelled checks or receipts for payment of 1st semester fees and expenses
- Financial aid and scholarship award letters from the college and/or independent sources
- Dormitory assignment letter
- Signed medical form (and other medical records if appropriate)
- Medical insurance information
- Registration form (and class schedule if sent in advance)
- Birth certificate or other proof of citizenship
- Social Security Number
- Emergency contact list

THEY'RE OFF!

After all the hard work and planning, the time for your student to leave for college will arrive before you know it. Whether they choose to travel on their own, or you accompany them to school; it is an occasion that marks a significant turning point in the parent-child relationship. Although you will still be an important source of emotional and financial support for your student, they will be assuming primary responsibility for making the day-to-day decisions that govern their lives. Learning to adjust to your student's growing independence and relating to them on an adult-to-adult basis are two of the biggest challenges that you will face as a parent. Here are some suggestions on how to approach this new phase in your relationship:

✔ *Communicate Regularly (Even If It's Often One-Way):* Receiving telephone calls and written communications is an important way for your student to stay connected with what is happening at home. You'll want to keep them informed about what family members are doing, as well as update them on the progress of sports teams or organizations they may have been involved in. From time to time, you may also want to send articles from your local newspaper or a favorite magazine that they might enjoy. You can also enlist other relatives and family friends to write or call your student periodically. Care packages containing homemade treats are especially welcome. The idea is to keep a regular flow of communications headed their way during the first few months away from home.

Don't expect a response to every card or letter that you write. Although they enjoy receiving mail, college students are immersed in their own activities and will rarely take time to write back. Electronic communications are typically preferred, so consider yourself lucky if you get a phone call or e-mail once in a while.

Rather than try to call your student at random, you may want to set up a regular time for a call from home. Allow your student to suggest a time that won't conflict with their activities, study hours and sleeping habits. What worked well for us was to schedule our weekly calls to Jason on Sunday evenings. Although he didn't always have a lot to say each time, he seemed to find it reassuring that we always checked in. We were even surprised to find that the few times that we didn't call at the appointed hour, he called us to see what happened.

Hint: There are a number of websites from which you can send free electronic greeting cards to your student. Most sites have a wide range of cards (from funny to sentimental) that are suitable for any occasion, and even allow you to specify a particular delivery date. This is an ideal way to let your student know that you are thinking of them.

✔ *Be Supportive, But Not Over Protective:* You'll want to let your student know that you are confident in their ability to succeed on their own, but also communicate that you are available when they need to talk about how things are going. Listen to their concerns, but resist the temptation to jump in and solve their problems. A better approach is to help them brainstorm possible solutions and direct them to on-campus resources that can assist with implementation (e.g. student counseling and health centers, deans, faculty advisors, resident advisors, office of academic support services, etc.). Be sure to also tell them that you are proud of the way they are taking responsibility for resolving their own problem.

Although you want to encourage your student to solve minor problems on their own, there may be times when it is necessary for you to get involved. Things to look out for include: prolonged homesickness; inability to adjust to the academic and social demands of college; evidence of serious illness or chronic fatigue; unusual weight loss; drastic behavioral changes or other signs of depression. If you suspect that there might be serious difficulty, contact the campus counseling service and ask them to request that your student come in for an evaluation. Follow up with them after the meeting to determine an appropriate course of action.

✔ *Demonstrate Interest:* Even though your student will be eager to establish their independence, they still want to know that their family is interested in them. By all means, encourage them to talk about classes and new friends—

but try to avoid being overly inquisitive and appearing to nag. Take advantage of opportunities to visit with your student in their new environment. These visits provide a chance to learn more about your student's life on campus and give them an opportunity to introduce you to their new friends and activities. You'll want to call ahead to see if the time will be convenient, since your student may already have plans that would be preempted by your visit. An ideal time to visit is during Parent's or Family Weekend, when there are special activities planned and your student's friends may have parents visiting also.

> **Hint**: Be sure to include a trip to a restaurant as part of your visit and give your student the opportunity to invite a friend or two. The place doesn't have to be fancy or expensive—just a change from the ordinary cafeteria fare. Your offer will be eagerly accepted, since most college students will appreciate the chance to eat some "real food" for a change.

✔ *Be Prepared for Change:* You will find that your student may explore a variety of social, attitudinal and behavioral options as a result of the many new ideas and experiences they will be exposed to at college. Don't be surprised if they suddenly develop new habits, interests or personality traits—or drop an activity that they have previously been committed to. Many freshmen also choose to express their emerging identity by using a different name or making noticeable changes in their physical appearance (e.g. hairstyles, style of clothing, body piercing, tattoos, etc.)

It can be hard for parents to adjust to these changes—especially if they appear to challenge family norms and values. However, unless a change represents a significant risk to your student's health and well-being, the best thing to do is to relax and take it in stride. Try to remember that beneath the new persona is the same child that you know and love. You'll likely find that some of the more extreme changes will be modified or left behind as your student matures and grows comfortable with his or her adult identity.

✔ *Enjoy Your Student's Visits Home:* The key to a pleasant visit is for both parties to be clear about rules and expectations. While your student may expect the same freedom that they have at college, it is likely that you will not be comfortable with that scenario. As you did during the previous summer, you'll need to strike a balance between respecting household rules and acknowledging your student's growing maturity and independence. Remember that your student will be anxious to spend time with friends, so be sure to book some "family time" on their schedule. Plan to include low-key family activities as well as special events during the time you spend together.

> **Hint**: Although you will be excited to have your student at home, resist the temptation to treat them like a guest. For example, they should be expected to do their part around the house, even though other family members have assumed their regular chores while they are away at school.

NOTES

_____

_____

_____

_____

_____

_____

_____

_____

NOTES

_____

_____

_____

_____

_____

_____

_____

_____

_____

_____

_____

_____

_____

_____

_____

_____

_____

_____

_____

_____

_____

A Final Thought

It has been said that there are two important gifts that parents can give their children: one is Roots, and the other is Wings. When you give your child the skills and opportunity to fly solo, chances are that they will always be eager to return home after their journeys. When they go off to college, you can continue to support them, understand them, trust them, and pray for them—but it is important that you also let go and let them soar!

APPENDIX

I. College Selection and Admissions Resources

Comprehensive Resource Guides *(available at major national bookstore chains)*

- *A is for Admission: The Insider's Guide to Getting into the Ivy League and Other Top Colleges* by Michele A. Hernandez. ©1999 Warner Books. ISBN 0446674060

- *College Countdown: The Parent's and Student's Survival Kit for the College Admissions Process* by Jill F. Von Gruben. ©1999 McGraw-Hill. ISBN 0071352902

- *College Planning for Dummies* by Pat Odovensky. ©1999 IDG Books Worldwide. ISBN 0764551647

- *Getting In: Inside the College Admissions Process* by William Henry Paul. ©1997 Perseus Press. ISBN 0201154919

- *Peterson's 4 Year Colleges* (2000 Edition): *The Best Advice, the Best Tools, the Right Guide.* ©1999 Peterson's Guides. ISBN 0768901944

- *Playing the Selective College Admissions Game* by Richard Moll. ©1994 Penguin USA. ISBN 0140513035

- *The Best 331 Colleges* (2000 Edition) edited by Edward T. Custard. ©1999 Princeton Review. ISBN 0375754113

- *The College Admissions Mystique* by Bill Mayher. ©1998 Noonday Press. ISBN 0374525137

- *The College Handbook* (2000 Edition) by The College Board. ©1999 College Entrance Examination Board. ISBN 0874476259

- *The Fiske Guide to Colleges* (2000 Edition) by Edward B. Fiske and Robert Logue. ©1999 Times Books. ISBN 0812931718

- *The Insider's Guide to the Colleges* (2000 Edition) by Yale Daily News staff. ©1999 Griffin Trade Paperback. ISBN 03122041

- *You're Gonna Love This College Guide* by Marty Nemko and Deborah Zembe. ©1999 Barrons Educational Series. ISBN 0764108166

INTERNET SOURCES

- **College Board Online** (www.collegeboard.org): includes SAT registration and test preparation; extensive college search database; financial aid and scholarship resources and on-line applications.

- **College Night** (www.collegenight.com): features a searchable database of colleges and universities and other information on the obtaining admission and financial aid.

- **College Quest** (www.collegequest.com): searchable databases of accredited colleges and universities as well as over $2.5 Billion in scholarship opportunities. Also features applications to over 1200 colleges and universities.

- **CollegeBound Network** (www.collegebound.net): provides information on the admissions process and college life. Site offers virtual college tours and financial aid information, among other features.

- **CollegeSource Online** (www.collegesource.org): provides full text college catalogs from colleges across the U.S.

- **CollegeView** (www.collegeview.com): on-line college search service with profiles and contact information for U.S. colleges and universities.

- **Common Application** (www.commonapp.org): see if the schools your student is interested in are among the more than 150 independent colleges and universities that accept this common application form. Saves time since the student essay and recommendations are copied and sent to each individual school.

- **E-Hound** (www.e-hound.org): allows you to send yourself reminders of important dates in the admission process.

- **Embark.com** (www.embark.com): comprehensive resource guide for applying to colleges and graduate schools over the Internet. Also features information on college life, convenient checklists and a store for purchasing items needed for college.

- **Go College** (www.gocollege.com): provides information on all aspects of the process of gaining admissions and obtaining financial aid.

- **Kaplan** (www.kaplan.com): SAT/ACT preparation information and college admissions advice are provided on this site.

II. Senior Year Expense List

- Campus visits
  - ✔ Transportation
  - ✔ Housing
  - ✔ Meals
  - ✔ Etc.
- Cap and Gown Rental
- College Application Fees
- Dances (Homecoming, Senior Prom, Sadie Hawkins, etc.)
  - ✔ clothing purchase or rental
  - ✔ dinner
  - ✔ transportation
  - ✔ photographs
  - ✔ etc.
- Deposits to confirm registration and housing for fall semester
- Graduation Announcements
- Graduation Gifts for your student and others that you know well
- Graduation Party or Open House
  - ✔ invitations
  - ✔ foods
  - ✔ decorations
  - ✔ entertainment
  - ✔ etc.
- Graduation Photos
  - ✔ Yearbook portrait
  - ✔ Prints to give family and friends
- Luggage
- Materials for Senior Display or Scrapbook
- Photo developing
- Postage for college applications, graduation announcements, party invitations, thank you notes, etc.
- SAT/ACT test preparation and registration fees

- Senior Class trip
- Senior Memorabilia
  - ✔ class ring or other jewelry
  - ✔ graduation tassel
  - ✔ class T-shirts
  - ✔ senior video
  - ✔ etc.
- Senior Party (planned activity following graduation ceremony; usually organized and funded by parents)
- Stationery for letters and thank you notes
- Yearbook

III. Financial Aid Resources

Comprehensive Resource Guides *(available in major national bookstore chains)*:

- *Cash for College* (Revised Edition) by Cynthia Ruiz McKee and Phillip C. McKee, Jr. ©1999 William Morrow. ISBN 0688161901

- *College Costs & Financial Aid Handbook* (2000 Edition) by The College Board. ©1999 College Entrance Examination Board. ISBN 0874476283

- *College Financial Aid for Dummies* by Herm Davis and Joyce Lain Kennedy. ©1999 IDG books Worldwide. ISBN 0764551655

- *How to Go to College Almost for Free* by Benjamin R. Kaplan. ©1999 Waggle-Dancer Books. ISBN 0933094302

- *Scholarships* (2000 Edition) by Gail Schlacter, R. David Weber and the Staff of Reference Service Press. ©1999 Kaplan Books. ISBN 0684866129

- *The "B" Student's Complete Scholarship Book (The Scholarship Book Where Grades Don't Matter)* by Student Services LLC. ©1997 Sourcebooks, Inc. ISBN 1570711445

- *The Complete Scholarship Book* (2nd Edition) by Student Services LLC. ©1998 Sourcebooks, Inc. ISBN 1570713901

- *The Scholarship Advisor* (2000 Edition) by Chris Vuturo. ©1999 Princeton Review Publishing. ISBN 0375754687

- *The Scholarship Book* (2000 Edition) by Daniel J. Cassidy. ©1999 Prentice Hall Press. ISBN 0735200793

- *U.S. Government Publications (available at no charge from the U.S. Department of Education, PO Box 84, Washington, DC 20044-0084 or call 1-800-433-3243)*
  - *Funding Your Education:* contains tips on applying for financial aid using the Free Application for Federal Student Aid form (FAFSA).

- *School Shopping Tips:* provides basic information about finding the right college and applying for financial aid.

- *The Student Guide to Financial Aid:* provides information on federal grants, loans and work-study programs.

INTERNET SOURCES

- *FastAid* (www.fastaid.com): one of the largest financial aid databases. Published by Dan Cassidy, author of "The Scholarship Book" resource guide.

- *FastWEB* (www.fastweb.com): searchable database of more than 400,000 scholarships that is updated daily. Provides a free personalized list of scholarship opportunities if you complete a detailed questionnaire containing information on your academic achievements, family background and income.

- *FinAid!* (www.finaid.com): database of information on loans, scholarships and military aid. Also includes financial aid calculators.

- *FreSch!* (www.freschinfo.com): database of more than 2000 sources of financial aid awards. Also features discussion forums on financial aid topics.

- *Minority On-Line Information Service* (www.fie.com/molis/scholar.htm): a searchable database of scholarships available for minority applicants.

- *SallieMae Scholarship Search* (http://scholarships.salliemae.com): service allows students to search the CASHE database for funding information from a variety of resources, including scholarships, fellowships, grants, work study, loan programs, tuition waivers, internships, competitions, and work co-operative programs. Search results e-mailed within 24 hours.

- *Scholarship Resource Network* (www.srnexpress.com): search engine and database of private scholarships. The award listings in the SRN database contain more detailed

information than can be found in most scholarship databases and scholarship listing books. SRN contains over
150,000 awards worth a total of more than $35 million.

- Most general college-related websites also have financial
  aid links. Some of the most popular include: College
  Board Online (www.collegeboard.org), CollegeNet
  (www.collegenet.com), GoCollege (www.gocollege.com),
  Embark.Com (www.embark.com), and Peterson's
  CollegeQuest (www.collegequest.com).

IV. Sample Student Activity Grid

Name: John B Davis, Jr.
Social Security #: 000-00-0000

Activities and Honors

Activity	Grade Level 9	10	11	12	Commentary (e.g. Positions Held, Honors, Awards)
Academic Achievement					
• AP Chemistry				✔	• Department Honors
• AP History				✔	
• Dean's Honors List	✔	✔	✔	✔	• Elected to National Honor Society (Senior Year)
• Biology Research Project (Univ. of MN)				✔	• Intel Science Talent Search applicant
Leadership					
• Student Council		✔	✔	✔	• Junior Class Representative; Senior Class Secretary
• Key Service Club	✔	✔	✔	✔	• Gold Key Service award (Senior Year)
• Church Youth Group	✔	✔	✔	✔	• Treasurer; Vice-President
Athletics					
• Varsity Track		✔	✔	✔	• Co-Captain; 3 Year Letterman; All-Conference (Senior Year)
• Jr. Varsity Track	✔				
• Varsity Basketball			✔	✔	• 2 Year Letterman
• Jr. Varsity Basketball	✔	✔			
Civic/Community					
• Cookie Cart			✔		• Worked with inner-city kids in a non-profit bakery operation
• Special Olympics Volunteer		✔	✔	✔	• Assisted in setting up athletic events; transported athletes to venues
• Toys for Tots Volunteer			✔	✔	• Distributed toys to inner-city families during Xmas holidays
Employment					
• Detail Center Employee at Car Wash	✔				• Summer only
• Host, Perkins Café		✔			• Summer & part-time during school year
• Retail Space Associate, Coca-Cola Bottling Co.			✔		• Summer only

V. COLLEGE PACKING CHECKLIST

Academic Supplies
- Address book
- Bookends
- Calculator
- Calendar
- Desk lamp
- Dictionary
- Drawer organizer
- Envelopes
- Erasers
- File folders
- Glue stick
- Highlighters
- Index cards
- Notebooks
- Notepaper
- Paper clips
- Paper punch
- Pencil holder
- Pencil sharpener
- Pens and pencils
- Post-it notes
- Rubber bands
- Scissors
- Scotch tape
- Stamps
- Staple remover
- Stapler & staples
- Stationery
- Tape measure
- Thesaurus
- Thumb tacks

Bedding/Linens
- Bedspread or comforter
- Blanket
- Mattress pad
- Pillows (2)
- Sheets & pillowcases
- Towels & washcloths (2–3)

Cleaning Supplies
- Air freshener
- Broom and dustpan
- Bucket and sponge
- Dishwashing detergent
- Goo-gone cleaner
- Paper towels
- Small dish pan
- Spray cleaner
- Spray disinfectant (e.g. Lysol)

Clothing Care
- Iron
- Lint remover brush
- Plastic hangars
- Portable ironing board
- Sewing kit

Health Items
- Antacid
- Antibiotic ointment
- Bandages
- Cold medicine
- Cotton balls
- Cough medicine
- First aid kit
- Multi-Vitamins
- Pain reliever
- Prescription medicines
- Sore throat spray
- Sunscreen
- Thermometer

Laundry Supplies
- Detergent
- Drying rack
- Fabric softener sheets
- Laundry bag
- Laundry instructions
- Spot remover (e.g. Shout)

Personal Care/Grooming
- Cologne
- Comb & brush
- Dental floss
- Deodorant
- Facial tissue
- Hair conditioner
- Hair dryer
- Hand & body lotion
- Makeup
- Mouthwash
- Nail clipper
- Q Tips
- Razor
- Shampoo
- Shaving cream
- Shower caddy
- Shower shoes/thongs
- Soap
- Toothbrush
- Toothpaste

Toolbox
- Door stop
- Duct tape
- Extension cords
- Flashlight & batteries
- Hammer
- Light bulbs
- Measuring tape
- Nails
- Packaging tape
- Pliers
- Screwdriver & screws
- Telephone cord

Computer Supplies
- Computer & lock
- Computer manuals
- Computer paper
- Ink cartridges
- Printer
- Surge protector

Food Accessories
- Bottle opener
- Can opener
- Food storage containers
- Garbage bags
- Hot pot (if allowed)
- Microwave (if allowed)
- Mugs
- Paper cups
- Paper plates
- Plastic bowls
- Plastic knives, forks and spoons
- Refrigerator
- Salt and pepper
- Water bottle

Miscellaneous
- Answering machine
- Camera & batteries
- CD player & CD's
- Clock radio w/alarm
- Combination lock
- Film

- Gym bag
- Playing cards
- Sports equipment
- Sunglasses
- Swimsuit
- Telephone
- Television/VCR
- Umbrella

Order Form

To purchase additional copies of *Surviving Senior Year* (ISBN 1-890676-73-X), please fill out the information below:

Name: _____

Address: _____

City/State/ZIP: _____

Daytime Telephone: _____

Number of Books _____ X $13.95 = _____

Shipping Per Book _____ X $2.00 = _____

Sales Tax Per Book _____ X $0.91 = _____
(MN residents only)

                             Total   = _____

Payable in U.S. Funds only. No cash/COD. Make checks or money orders payable to **Waterford Marketing Group**.

Please allow 4-6 weeks for U.S. delivery.

Mail your order to:
Waterford Marketing Group
P.O. Box 27383
Golden Valley, MN 55427

Special quantity discounts available for sales promotions, premiums, or fund-raising use. For details, please write to Waterford Marketing Group at the address listed above or send a FAX to 763-302-9262. Include estimated quantity and timing required, along with the name and telephone number of a contact person.

Have You Found This Guidebook To Be Helpful?

We need your input to improve the quality and usefulness of *Surviving Senior Year*. We would greatly appreciate your thoughts and suggestions regarding this guidebook, as well as any ideas you have about additional topics you'd like to see covered in future editions.

Thank you in advance for your feedback.

1. Overall, how would you rate your level of satisfaction with *Surviving Senior Year*?

    Please circle your response.

    Extremely Dissatisfied   Satisfied   Extremely Satisfied

         1   2   3   4   5

2. What section(s) of the book did you find most helpful?

    _____

    _____

    _____

    _____

    _____

    _____

3. What section(s) did you find least helpful?

    _____

    _____

    _____

    _____

    _____

    _____

4. What additional topics do you think should be included in future editions of *Surviving Senior Year*?

_____

_____

_____

_____

_____

5. Do you have a few helpful senior year hints of your own? (Feel free to use additional sheets if necessary).

_____

_____

_____

_____

_____

_____

Name (optional):_____

Address:_____

City/State/ZIP:_____

Telephone: _____

Please Mail Your Response to:

Waterford Marketing Group,
PO Box 27383
Golden Valley, MN 55427

or Fax to: (763) 302-9262

ABOUT THE AUTHOR

Linda Keene is the proud mother of a recent high school graduate. She applied many of the organizational skills honed as a successful marketing executive to the challenge of helping her family cope with the many demands associated with her son's last year of high school. Her goal in writing this book is to provide other parents with information and ideas that can make the entire process more manageable—and enjoyable.

Linda received her undergraduate degree from Boston University School of Management, from which she received the Distinguished Alumni Award in 1999. She also holds an MBA from Harvard University School of Business Administration. She is currently employed by a Fortune 100 diversified financial services company and has been recognized by *Essence, Ebony* and *Black Enterprise* magazines as one of America's top corporate African-American women.

Linda is a native of New York City. She currently resides in Minneapolis, Minnesota, with her husband, Robert. Their son, Jason, is a student at Morehouse College in Atlanta, Georgia.